An introduction to playing and understanding the drum kit

By Dave Hazlewood

Foundation level

Music by Dan Wright - Edited by Rob Woodcock

PUBLISHING

Knowle Farm Business Centre, Wadhurst Road,
Frant, Tunbridge Wells, Kent, TN3 9EJ
United Kingdom
www.one8e.co.uk • info@one8e.co.uk

ISBN 978-0-9567790-2-1

Backbone drums – Foundation level
This volume: 2nd edition
© Copyright 2013 Dave Hazlewood

Dave Hazlewood has asserted his right
to be identified as the author of this work
in accordance with the Copyright,
Designs and Patents Act 1988

Produced by one8e publishing
Published by one8e publishing
All rights reserved

Printed by The Printing House, London, England, W1S 1YH

Edited by Rob Woodcock
Music by Dan Wright
Cover design by Andy McIntosh
Additional technical input from Mike Brazier
Cover photography by Mark Roe and David Brown
Internal photography by Mark Roe and Dan Wright

CREATE GREAT MUSICIANS, NOT JUST EXAM PASSES!

BackBone DRUMS
ON-LINE LESSON MANAGEMENT

Teachers can save time and effort while continuing to improve the quality of their drum lessons by using our very own lesson manager software.

Developed to fully compliment the Backbone Drums teaching syllabus, run your entire teaching practice and keep track of all of your students contact informaton and progress with one easy to use programme.

Motivate and encourage students by recording all progress and achievements within their very own profile page. Use each students individual drummer score and progress chart to help them develop in all areas of their playing.

Create, print and save bespoke lesson and practice plans. See at a glance what each student is working on and where they are within the syllabus, then make simple notes throughout each lesson to record topics covered and plan ideas for their next lesson.

Spend less time planning and more time playing!

THE COMPLETE SOFTWARE SOLUTION FOR DRUM TEACHERS

www.backbonedrums.com

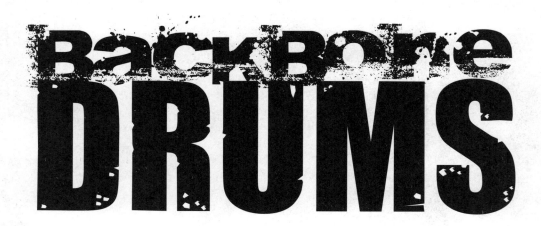

Welcome to Backbone Drums, Foundation

This book covers all of the basic elements of playing drums. Once completed, you will know the role you play as a drummer within a band, be able to play a variety of simple beats and fills in time, develop your own ideas and understand how the drum kit works as a musical instrument.

Your 'Backbone' of knowledge

Drums are the backbone of any band and the drummer plays a vital part in making it successful.
This series of books is designed to be the backbone of a drummer's knowledge by looking into a huge number of concepts, techniques and styles which build in complexity as the series progresses.

Created for the real world of drumming

With many years of professional drumming experience gigging, touring, recording and teaching, these books have been written with integrity and arranged in a logical order to give students the most fun yet practical drum lessons.

This is not just about passing exams!

www.backbonedrums.com

Contents

Backing track list

Backing tracks - Suitable for exercises from chapters one - five
01 60bpm Pop ballad
02 65bpm Rock ballad
03 70bpm Piano ballad
04 75bpm Pop rock
05 80bpm Dream pop
06 85bpm Nineties rock
07 90bpm Classic rock
08 95bpm Grunge rock
09 100bpm Light pop
10 105bpm Glam rock
11 110bpm Bubblegum pop
12 115bpm Eighties rock
13 120bpm Funky pop

Chart tracks - To accompany the charts from chapter six
14 Chart 2 with drums
15 Chart 2 with click
16 Chart 3 with drums
17 Chart 3 with click
18 Chart 4 with drums
19 Chart 4 with click

Click tracks – Suitable for exercises from any chapter (loop each track)
20 Click @ 60bpm
21 Click @ 65bpm
22 Click @ 70bpm
23 Click @ 75bpm
24 Click @ 80bpm
25 Click @ 85bpm
26 Click @ 90bpm
27 Click @ 95bpm
28 Click @ 100bpm
29 Click @ 105bpm
30 Click @ 110bpm
31 Click @ 115bpm
32 Click @ 120bpm

BPM – Beats Per Minute
Speed in music is called 'Tempo' and is measured in 'beats per minute'. All backing tracks contain a click which marks this time and occur on every quarter note.

Throughout this book you will often see 'bpm' written to either give you an idea of how fast you are playing or to give you goals to work towards.

Backing track guide

The first part of the audio CD contains backing tracks for you to play along with when completing exercises from this book. There are several ways to use these tracks, which will become more apparent the further you get through the book.

Groove playing
Initially looping one exercise along with a track will help to develop your timing and will be a great way to gauge your progress.

Four bar phrasing
Each section in all backing tracks is written in groups of four bars, so you're able to loop four bar phrases all the way through a track and feel where the sections change without getting out of sync with the song.

Song structures
All of the backing tracks have the same structure.

A – Four bars – Intro/bridge (or extended chorus)
B – Four bars – Verse (part 1)
B – Four bars – Verse (part 2)
C – Four bars – Chorus

This arrangement is repeated four times.

Listen to the backing tracks to hear how the music changes from section to section, and then see how you can play each song more musically by playing a different groove for each section and fills that help move between them.

Chart writing
This is your chance to be really creative by writing drum parts and will be a great exercise to prepare you for playing with a real band. If, by the end of this book, you are totally happy with reading music, you could have a go at writing your own ideas in the form of a chart! Remember the arrangement (ABBC) is repeated four times and each time through doesn't have to be the same. Only attempt this if you are completely happy with everything in this book and you are working with a drum teacher, as this will be difficult to complete on your own with no guidance!

Reading and rudiment practice
Although the click tracks (20 – 32) are ideal for practicing reading exercises or rudiments, it's a good idea to play the rudiments along with the musical backing tracks as well. Playing a paradiddle or double stroke roll along with a rock track at 90bpm, will be more interesting than playing to just a click at 90bpm and will help you to develop a more musical feel.

Book guide

When giving note values their names, we have used a more modern system using fractions as names instead of giving them their more classical names. Although you don't need to know the classical names to work through this book, they are still used in certain situations so it's a good idea to learn them.

• Whole note – Semi-breve
• Half note – Minim
• Quarter note – Crotchet
• Eighth note – Quaver
• Sixteenth note – Semi Quaver

Note positions
The position of each drum and cymbal within the stave can vary in different publications as there has never been a universal standard. The positions used in this book have been the most common for most drummers and authors for some time now.

The stems of notes in written music can go up or down depending on where they sit on the stave. In drum music this is not always the case, but instead are written to be as easy to follow as possible.

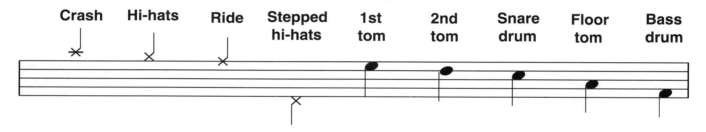

Left-handed drummers
Any exercise in this book that requires either a left or right hand to play a specific note has been written from a right-handed player's point of view. Left-handed players should reverse any instructions that state left and right.

Hi-hats or ride
Most of the grooves in this book are written with the cymbal part played on the hi-hats. A lot of these grooves will work just as well if played on the ride, so feel free to experiment.

Signing off and moving on
At the bottom of most pages within this book and the rest of the series, you will see a section titled 'Signing off and moving on'. These have targets that you should aim to achieve before moving on. They are broken down into Bronze, Silver and Gold; with Bronze being the minimum requirement, Silver being acceptable and Gold being a good standard at which to progress. Faster is not always better though, so make sure you sign off each target. Although it's preferable to sign off at Gold standard before moving on, it's not essential, and if you are struggling with any section, you should just make a note of what level you have achieved and move on. You can always go back to review weaker sections at a later date.

Teachers subscribing to the online lesson manager application will be able to record Gold, Silver and Bronze awards for each student using the progress records. These will show at a glance which areas need more attention and practice.

In the beginning

Quarter note (Crotchet)

In Chapter One, we look at the very basics of playing drums and how important the 'pulse' in music and counting is for a drummer.

Checklist

By the end of this chapter, you should be able to achieve the following:

- Name all the parts of the drum kit
- Explain the main job of a drummer in a band
- Name all the drum and cymbal positions on a stave
- Explain what a repeat sign means
- Explain what a groove is
- Explain what a fill is
- Play a quarter note groove
- Play quarter note fills
- Play four bar phrases
- Play along with backing tracks
- Create your own fills and play in four bar phrases

Use this page as an end-of-chapter test. When you have completed Chapter One, come back to this page and see if you can complete the list above.

CHAPTER ONE

Drum kit recognition

A drum kit is made up of drums and cymbals. The picture above is of a standard five-piece drum kit. Five-piece refers to the number of drums only and does not include cymbals or stands. In a standard five-piece drum kit there is a bass drum (sometimes refered to as a 'kick drum'), a snare drum and three tom toms (normally just called 'toms') known as either 1st, 2nd and floor toms or high, mid and low toms.

The cymbals shown here include a pair of hi-hats, a ride cymbal and two crash cymbals. The other bits (not labelled) that make up the drum kit are the hi-hat stand, snare stand and two cymbal stands. There will also be a drum stool to sit on.

• Please note that the hi-hat pedal is not used at this level, but will be introduced in the level one book.

Signing off and moving on
Name all drums and cymbals on your own drum kit correctly

Drum kit basic notation

To play and understand the exercises in this book, you will need to understand from the beginning a bit about how music is written and presented. This will not only help your learning, but is also an introduction to the knowledge required to be a great musician.

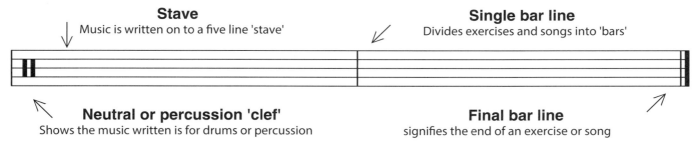

Stave
Music is written on to a five line 'stave'

Single bar line
Divides exercises and songs into 'bars'

Neutral or percussion 'clef'
Shows the music written is for drums or percussion

Final bar line
signifies the end of an exercise or song

Here are the most basic elements of reading music but you will learn more as you progress. Where a note is situated on the stave tells us which drum or cymbal to play. As a rough guide, 'the higher up the stave, the higher up the drum kit.' This is only a general rule and will depend slightly on how you set up your drums.

A cross written on the stave lets you know that you need to hit something metal (i.e. cymbals).

Crash   **Hi-hats**   **Ride**   **Stepped hi-hats**

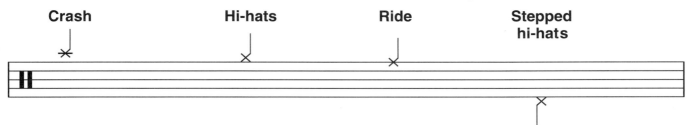

A dot on the stave lets you know to play a drum.

1st tom   **2nd tom**   **Snare drum**   **Floor tom**   **Bass drum**

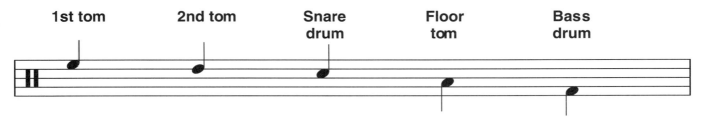

A drum kit is made up of two instruments, drums and cymbals. When drum kit music is written, it is quite often written as two parts. This is shown in the example below where the cymbal pattern is written above the drum pattern.

Signing off and moving on
Correctly identify where each drum and cymbal sits on a stave

Quarter note groove

Music on any instrument is broken up into bars, just as speech is broken up into words. Below is one bar of drum music where you will play the hi-hats, bass drum and snare drum. Your lead (stronger) hand plays the hi-hats four times, while your lead (stronger) foot and opposite hand alternate playing the bass drum and snare drum. The first and third hi-hats are played in time with the bass drum, while the second and fourth hi-hats are played in time with the snare.

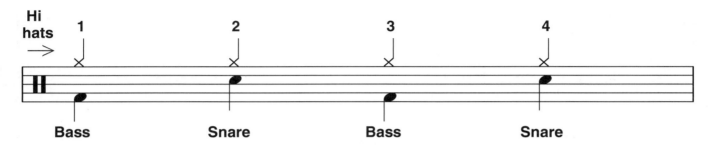

What you have just played is a basic 'groove' (also known as a 'beat' or 'rhythm'). A drummer's primary job is to keep time for a band and this is usually done by playing a groove over and over again in time with the pulse of the music. The pulse is the regular feel in music that you feel yourself tapping along to when listening to music, and is highlighted by the click sound within the backing tracks provided.

When you are comfortable with this groove, loop (repeat) it and play along with backing tracks.

Quarter note fill

Different sections of a song may have different types of grooves, so to help flow from one section to another, drummers also play fills. Below is a basic fill using the snare drum, first tom, second tom and floor toms. Play each beat with your lead hand.

Alternate playing the groove and then the fill at the same speed without speeding up or slowing down.

Signing off and moving on
Play the quarter note groove along with suitable backing tracks
Targets are in BPM

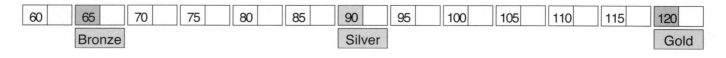

Quarter note four bar phrase

Fills are played far less often than grooves and you may play long sections with no fills at all. Because of this you need to know that when you do play a fill, it is in the correct place.

Most modern music is written in sections, which are quite often in groups of four bars, so practicing playing fills in every fourth bar, will get you used to how that feels and make it easier to incorporate fills into your playing. This is known as a four bar phrase (three bars of groove and one bar of fill) and is written out below. Note that the first bar of groove now starts with a crash instead of a hi-hat. This works well when coming out of the fill and going back into the groove when repeating.

The count above the stave may seem a little strange to begin with, but this is the best way to count when playing multiple bars as the first number of each bar tells you which bar you are in. It's worth practicing to get this right!

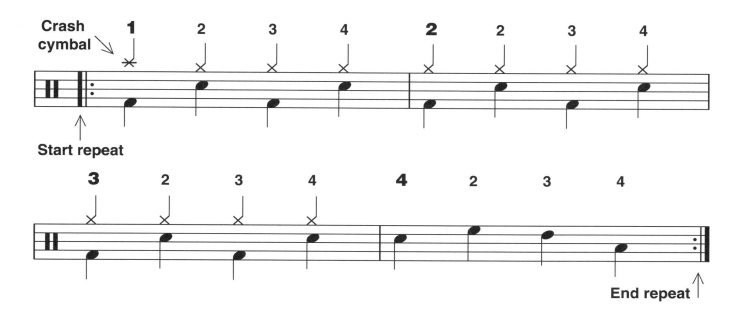

Crash cymbal: Play a crash cymbal instead of a hi-hat at the start of each four bar phrase.

Start repeat/end repeat: When you see these bar lines, you are required to play everything between them for a second time. When you get to the 'end repeat' sign, go back to the 'start repeat' sign and play through again. If there is an 'end repeat' sign, but no 'start repeat' sign, you go back to the start of the piece.

When you are comfortable with this exercise play every other four bar phrase on the ride cymbal instead of the hi-hats.

Signing off and moving on
Play the above four bar phrase along with suitable backing tracks
Targets are in BPM

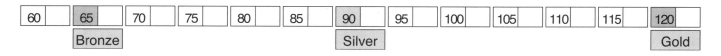

60		65		70		75		80		85		90		95		100		105		110		115		120
		Bronze										Silver												Gold

More fill ideas

Now that you have mastered playing the quarter note groove and fill in four bar phrases, here are some fill variations to make things a bit more interesting. Start slowly and play four bar phrases with a backing track when you feel comfortable.

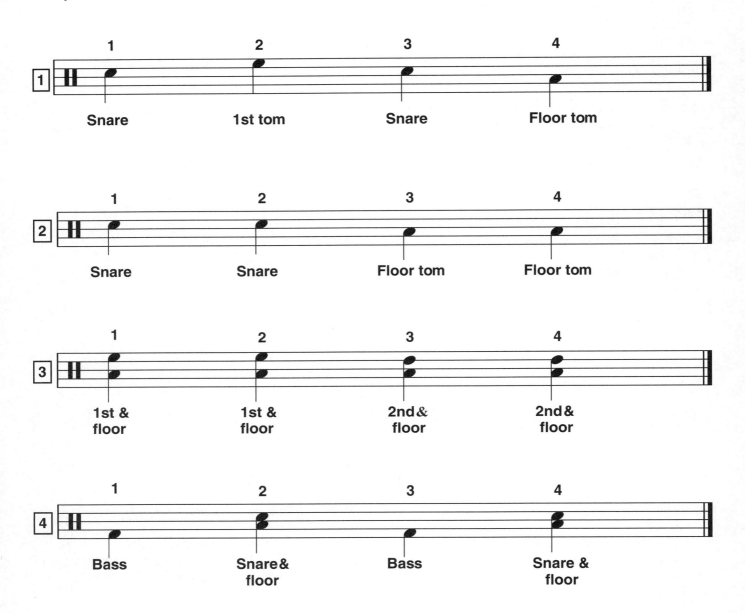

Signing off and moving on

Play all fills in four bar phrases along with backing tracks
Targets are in BPM

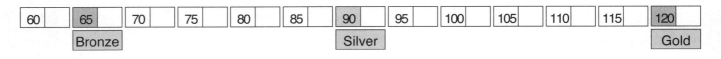

Create your own fills using quarter notes

Now it's your turn! Use the blank manuscript below to make your own fills. Be as creative as you want, but make sure you keep your fills in time. Write the notes on the correct lines, but if possible don't write the drum names as this will help you learn where each drum and cymbal sits on the stave.

Signing off and moving on
Play all fills in four bar phrases along with backing tracks
Targets are in BPM

60	65	70	75	80	85	90	95	100	105	110	115	120
	Bronze					Silver						Gold

Notes

Then there were eight

**Eighth note
(Quaver)**

**Two eighth notes
(Two quavers)**

**Four eighth notes
(Four quavers)**

In Chapter Two, we will look at playing eighth notes in grooves and fills and start to get more creative with the bass drum. A single eighth note looks different from a quarter note in that it has a 'tail'. When you get two or four eighth notes together they join their tails (see above).

Checklist

By the end of this chapter, you should be able to achieve the following:

- Play eighth note grooves
- Play eighth note fills
- Read music containing quarter notes and eighth notes
- Play fills mixing quarter notes and eighth notes
- Create your own fills mixing quarter notes and eighth notes
- Play quarter and eighth notes as snare and bass drum patterns
- Play varied snare and bass patterns with eighth note hi-hats
- Play varied snare and bass patterns with quarter note hi-hats
- Create your own grooves
- Understand what a time signature is and what 4/4 means

Use this page as an end-of-chapter test. When you have completed Chapter Two, come back to this page and see if you can complete the list above.

Eighth note groove

This next groove is similar to the first in that the snare and bass pattern is exactly the same, but the hi-hat pattern has changed. Your lead (stronger) hand is now playing twice as many hi-hats, which means there's an extra stroke in between each count. To help count and play this we will say 'and' (written as '+') in between our count. Because you are playing more notes, you may need to play this groove a bit slower to start.

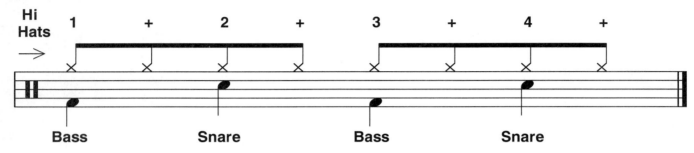

When you are comfortable with this groove, play it along with a backing track. Experiment playing the groove on the ride instead of the hi-hats.

Eighth note fill

As well as using eighth notes in grooves, we can play them in fills. Below is a basic fill using eighth notes. When you feel comfortable, alternate between the groove and fill, maintaining a steady tempo.

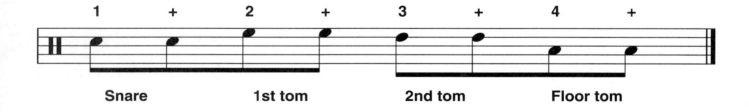

Signing off and moving on
Play the eighth-note groove along with suitable backing tracks
Targets are in BPM

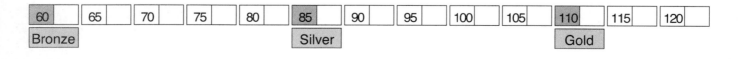

60	65	70	75	80	85	90	95	100	105	110	115	120
Bronze					Silver					Gold		

Eighth note four bar phrase

Just as we did with the quarter note groove and fill, we are going to play the eighth note groove and fill in four bar phrases along with backing tracks. When you are comfortable with this exercise have a go at playing every other four bar phrase on the ride cymbal instead of the hi-hats.

There is now a new symbol at the start of the piece which is explained below. You will also notice that there is an end repeat sign, but no start repeat sign. When this happens, you are expected to return to the start of the piece.

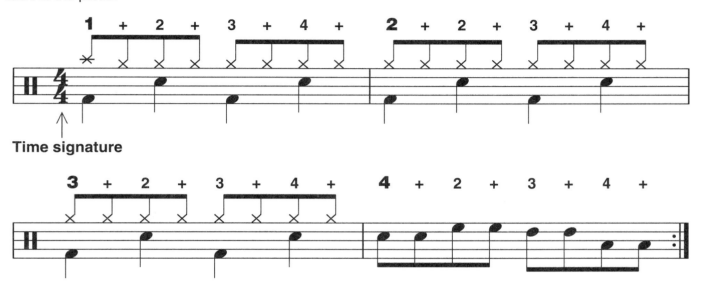

Time signature

Time signature

A time signature is something you will always see at the start of a piece of music and tells you about the timing and feel of the piece you are about to play.

The top number tells you how many counts are in a bar. (4 = Count up to four in each bar)
The bottom number tells you what type of note it is that you are counting. (4 = Quarter notes)

All of the exercises in this book are in 4/4 time which is the most common time signature used and is sometimes simply written as 'C' for 'Common time'.

There are several different time signatures and they can be read as if they were fractions:

4/4 = four quarter notes per bar.
3/4 = three quarter notes per bar.
6/8 = six eighth notes per bar.

Don't worry if this is a bit confusing, 4/4 will be the only time signature we shall be using for now.

Signing off and moving on
Play the above four bar phrase along with suitable backing tracks
Targets are in BPM

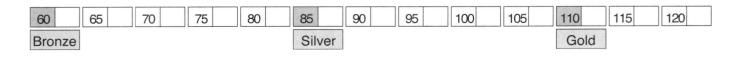

60		65	70	75	80	85	90	95	100	105	110	115	120
Bronze						Silver					Gold		

Reading exercises for the snare drum

We have looked at quarter notes and eighth notes on their own, but it is possible to mix them up within one bar. By mixing different notes within one bar, you can create some interesting rhythms. With all reading exercises like this, make sure you follow these few simple rules to aid learning and develop timing.

- Make sure you have a strong and even count – count out loud
- Play with a click track or metronome
- Tap your foot in time with the click track to help with timing
- Follow the suggested 'sticking' - R = Right (lead) hand L = Left (following) hand

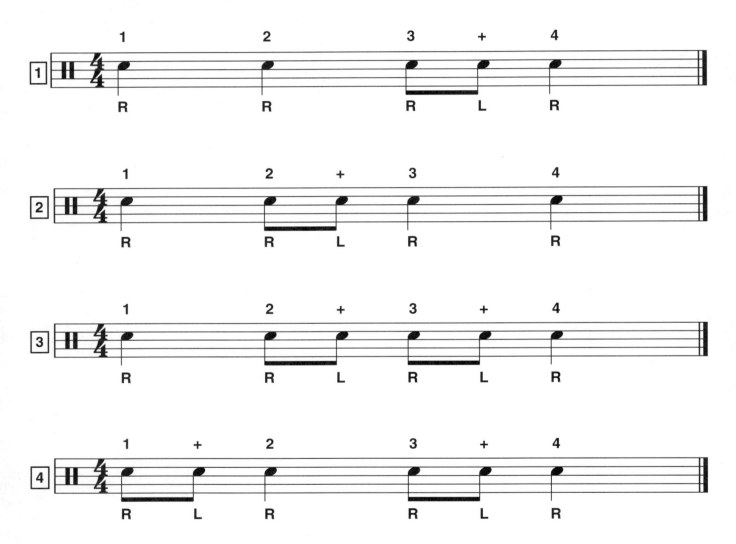

Signing off and moving on

Play the entire page as one exercise with a click track
Targets are in BPM

60	65	70	75	80	85	90	95	100	105	110	115	120
Bronze						Silver						Gold

Reading exercises played as fills

Now you are comfortable with the timing of playing quarter notes and eighth notes together, we can take the same rhythms and play them around the drums as fills.

Play the following fills slowly on their own to make sure you are playing the correct rhythms, and then using either the quarter note or the eighth note groove play them as fills in four bar phrases.

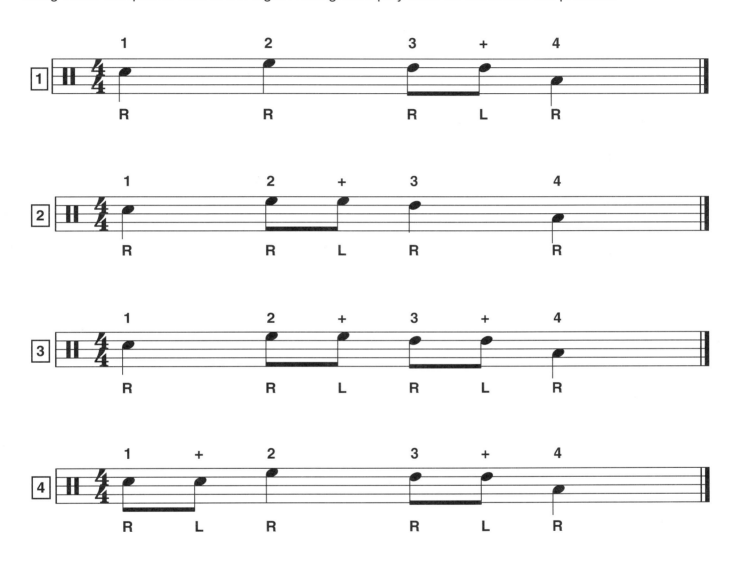

Signing off and moving on

Play each of the fills above in four bar phrases along with suitable backing tracks
Targets are in BPM

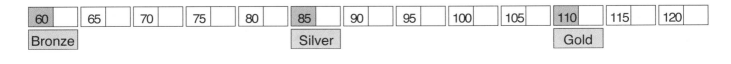

Create your own rhythms and fills

Use the blank staves below to make your own rhythms, which you can then play as fills. Write each exercise as a snare drum pattern and play as a reading exercise with a click. Only when you are comfortable with each of your ideas, play them around the drums as fills with quarter, or eighth note grooves in four bar phrases.

Use the following rhythms:

Quarter notes   Eighth notes

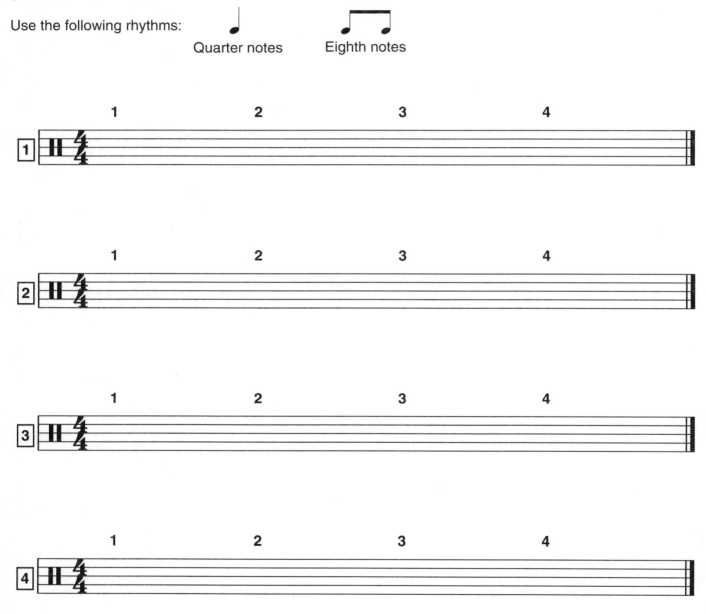

Signing off and moving on

Play each of the fills above in four bar phrases along with suitable backing tracks
Targets are in BPM

60		65		70		75		80		85		90		95		100		105		110		115		120	

Bronze	Silver	Gold

Quarter and eighth notes as snare and bass drum patterns

We have mixed quarter and eight notes to create new fills but we can also play them between the snare and bass drum to create some more interesting grooves. Here are the same four rhythms from page 12 but now split between the bass drum and snare drum as follows.

- Only the notes that fall on counts 2 and 4 are played on the snare drum.
- All other notes played on the bass drum

Play the following four exercises with no hi-hats. Don't play the snare drum with your lead hand though as this will be needed to play hi-hats when we add them.

Signing off and moving on
Play each of the patterns above with click tracks
Targets are in BPM

60	65	70	75	80	85	90	95	100	105	110	115	120
Bronze				Silver				Gold				

Snare and bass drum patterns with eighth note hi-hats

The following four grooves combine the previous snare drum and bass drum exercises with an eighth note hi-hat pattern. The grooves will sound similar to the first eighth note groove you played from page 10, but have extra bass drums, which will make them sound more interesting and musical.

A common way to make drum grooves work within music is to follow the rhythms played by other instruments with the bass drum. Listen to some rock or pop tunes to hear how the drum pattern works with the other instruments.

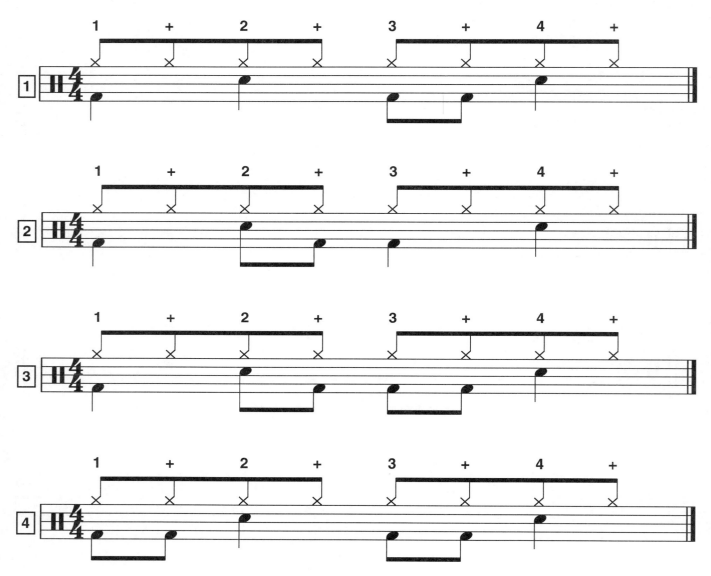

Signing off and moving on
Play each groove along with suitable backing tracks
Targets are in BPM

60		65		70		75		80		85		90		95		100		105		110		115		120	
Bronze										Silver										Gold					

Independence grooves

Independent means not dependent or influenced by anything else. An independent limb is therefore not dependent on or influenced by any other limb. This means that through study and practice we can have four limbs working independently of each other being able to play four completely different things. When you first play these grooves you may find you automatically play a hi-hat with the bass drums on the '+' count, but as your independence improves you will find your hi-hat hand will play consistent quarter notes whatever bass drum pattern you play.

The next four grooves combine the snare drum and bass drum exercises from page 15. Play each one individually with backing tracks and then play some four bar phrases using the fills from page 13.

Signing off and moving on
Play each groove along with suitable backing tracks
Targets are in BPM

Create your own grooves

Now have a go at making some grooves of your own. Write some snare and bass patterns into the four exercises below. You can use the rhythms you created on page 14 or make some new rhythms.

Remember:
- Only the notes that fall on counts two and four are played on the snare drum.
- All other notes are played on the bass drum.

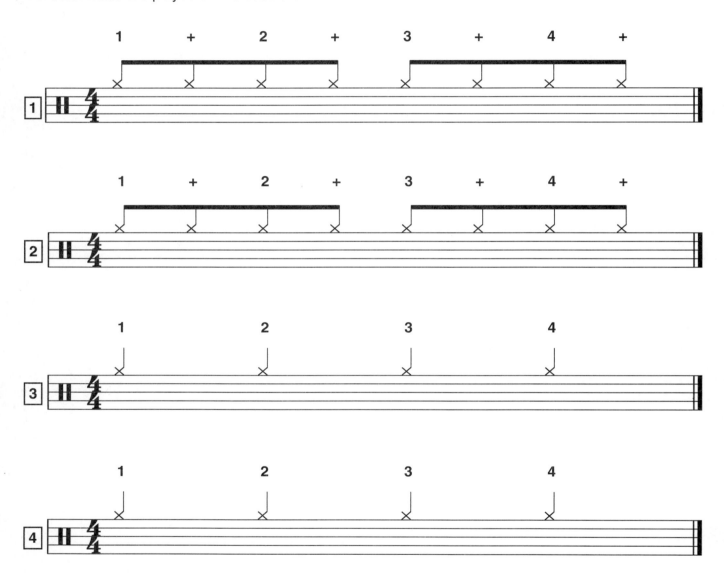

Signing off and moving on
Play each of your own grooves along with suitable backing tracks
Targets are in BPM

| 60 | | 65 | | 70 | | 75 | | 80 | | 85 | | 90 | | 95 | | 10u | | 105 | | 110 | | 115 | | 120 | |
| Bronze | | | | | | | | | | Silver | | | | | | | | | | Gold | | | | | |

That's the way to do it

In the first two chapters we have learnt to play different grooves and fills, but with any musical instrument how we play something is just as important as what we play. It is very important to remember that it is far better to play something simple and well executed, rather than something complicated and poorly executed.

Checklist

By the end of this chapter, you should be able to achieve the following:

- Explain the importance of good technique within your playing
- Demonstrate good posture
- Demonstrate good grip
- Demonstrate good bass drum technique
- Explain what rudiments are and why we practice them
- Play nice and even single stroke rolls with a click track
- Play nice and even double stroke rolls with a click track
- Play nice and even paradiddles with a click track
- Apply rudiments to fills

As in previous chapters, use this page as an end-of-chapter test. When you have completed Chapter Three, come back and see if you can complete the list above.

What is technique

Technique is the way we execute something and will make the following improvements to our playing:

- Better sound from the drums and cymbals
- Improved even placement of notes
- Louder when needed
- Quieter when needed
- Faster when needed
- Slower when needed
- Improved timing
- Improved musicality
- Good technique will also help to avoid injury and will require less energy

Good technique checklist:

Relax: Tension is your enemy!
If there is tension anywhere in your body, it will spread and work against you.
Make sure you are totally relaxed when playing and everything will sound better and happen much easier.

Good posture: Sit up straight and pull your shoulders back – DO NOT slouch or lean over your drum kit. Avoid looking at the ground when you play, but instead keep your head up.

Good grip: Anyone can pick up a bit of wood and hit a drum, but it takes a bit more work to do it well. Initially, you may find that your grip doesn't affect your playing, so why practice to improve it? As you progress and want to play more complicated and exciting drum parts, you will need complete control over your drum sticks and this can only be achieved with good grip. You might as well start getting it right now!

Which grip for me?

With many techniques that we use as drummers, there are quite often variations and options available to us. Some techniques help us to express ourselves in a certain way, whereas others are just personal preference. Watch a few top drummers playing and you will notice that they don't all play in exactly the same way, but instead all have individual styles.

There are several main variations of grip and there is no reason why you shouldn't learn and use more than one. There are three main variations looked at in this chapter, but we recommend that initially you start with 'German matched grip' as this is thought to be the strongest and most practical for beginners.

Each grip is made up of two elements, the front and the back of the grip.
• The front of the grip is called the 'fulcrum', which is where the stick can pivot between the thumb and first finger.
• The back of the grip is where the fingers control the stick, so initially they should always have contact with the stick.
Both elements of the grip need to be observed to gain complete control of the drum sticks.

Traditional grip: This grip goes back to the early days of military marching bands. Each hand holds the stick differently. The lead hand holds the stick from the top and the other hand holds the stick from underneath. This originally helped a marching drummer play over the side of his drum, which would be carried at an angle. Traditional grip is still used today by lots of drummers and is especially popular with jazz drummers.

Matched Grip: The most common modern grip is the matched grip where both hands hold the stick in the same way. This aids movement around a modern drum kit and is easier to learn. There are several variations of matched grip, here are the two most popular.

Matched Grip (French): With this version of matched grip, the palms of the hands face into each other and the fingers are used a lot to help move the stick. This is a common grip, but some say it lacks power due to the use of fingers more than the wrist.

Matched Grip (German): With German matched grip, the palms of the hands face down to the floor rather than into each other. This allows more movement in the wrist and can achieve a lot of power especially when combined with the use of the fingers.

Foot technique

We have looked at upper body technique, so we also need to look at technique for our feet. Many people spend a massive amount of time developing their hand technique, but tend to overlook their feet, which can lead to a playing imbalance.

Here are the two main variations:

As with grip, there are various options available to us for our foot technique. Again, some choices are down to personal preference, but there are different techniques for different jobs. For example, one technique will help you play faster, whereas a different technique may help you to play quieter. Initially, I would suggest comfort as a deciding factor to getting your foot technique working for you. We will revisit this subject in future books.

Heel down: This is a very relaxed technique, as your foot is left resting on the pedal with all of the work being done by your ankle. This is a good technique that gives a good open sound from the bass drum but can make playing very fast or very loud a bit trickier.

Heel up: This is a very powerful technique as the weight of your leg gets behind each stroke. This is a better technique for playing louder, but is not so relaxed. You can also get a much deader sound from a bass drum because the bass drum beater tends to stay pushed (or 'buried') into the drum head. With this technique, you may find it difficult to play softer.

Summary: With all of these hand and foot techniques, you should use what works for you. Some techniques will take longer to master, so don't be too quick to dismiss them. Remember to stay relaxed and make sure that whatever techniques you use, you don't put any stress on your joints, and if something hurts, stop and review what you are doing straight away.

What are rudiments?

Rudiments are basic exercises that all drummers need to practice to improve technique and general playing. They focus on the details of how we play, so that when we return to the drum kit we naturally play better. Although traditionally played as hand exercises, they can also be played with your feet or between hands and feet, so feel free to experiment. Practice all rudiments with a click track or backing tracks.

Note: Notice now, for the purposes of this book we will use a single line stave for rudiment exercises.

Single-stroke roll: one stroke with each hand

This is the first rudiment to practice and is very simple to learn. You have already been playing this rudiment when you played eighth note fills, so you can see how rudiments directly relate to what we play on the drum kit.

Double-stroke roll: two strokes with each hand

This rudiment is also very simple to learn but may take a bit more concentration to play consistently. Practice slowly to get used to the sticking and make sure that all notes are evenly placed.

Paradiddle: mixing single and double strokes

This rudiment mixes single and double strokes together, so will require a bit of practice to master. The paradiddle gets its name from the way it sounds when played, (PA-RA-DI-DDLE). Saying this as you play may help you learn. Make sure that this rudiment sounds as even as the single and double stroke rolls.

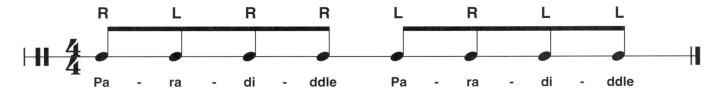

Signing off and moving on
Play each rudiment for at least one minute with a click track
Targets are in BPM

60	65	70	75	80	85	90	95	100	105	110	115	120
Bronze						Silver						Gold

Rudiments in fills

Having played these rudiments on just one drum, it is important to apply them to the drum kit so that we understand why we are spending our precious time practicing them. Here are a few ideas of how to apply rudiments to fills.

Double stroke rolls

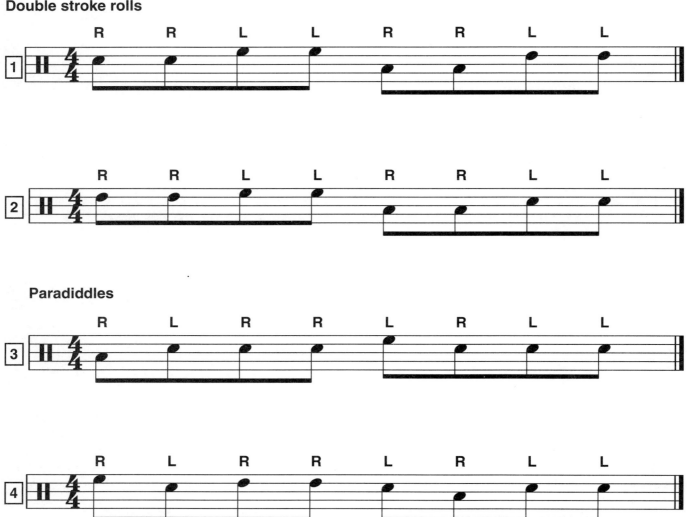

Paradiddles

When you are comfortable with these fills, experiment with some of your own ideas.

Signing off and moving on

Play each of the fills above with any groove in four bar phrases along with suitable backing tracks
Targets are in BPM

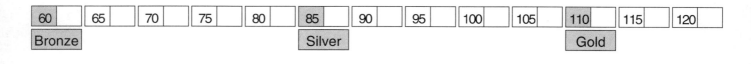

60		65	70	75	80	85	90	95	100	105	110	115	120
Bronze						Silver					Gold		

Mind the gap

Whole note   **Half note**   **Rests**
(Semi-breve)   **(Minim)**

We have now played grooves and fills with music, learnt about good technique and practiced some rudiments. It's now time to learn a bit of the theory to continue our development and create some space in our playing.

Checklist

By the end of this chapter, you should be able to achieve the following:

- Understand what a note value is
- Identify and state the value of whole, half, quarter and eighth notes
- Identify and state the value of whole, half, quarter and eighth note rests
- Read and play exercises containing whole, half, quarter and eight notes along with their respective rests
- Play fills that contain rests with various grooves in four bar phrases
- Play shorter fills that last less than one bar

As in previous chapters, use this page as an end-of-chapter test. When you have completed Chapter Four, come back to this page and see if you can complete this list.

CHAPTER FOUR

Note values

So far, we have been playing quarter and eighth notes in our grooves and fills. To understand them properly we need to look at them in a bit more detail.

All notes have a value and they get their names from their relationship to a note called a 'whole note' which has the greatest value of them all.

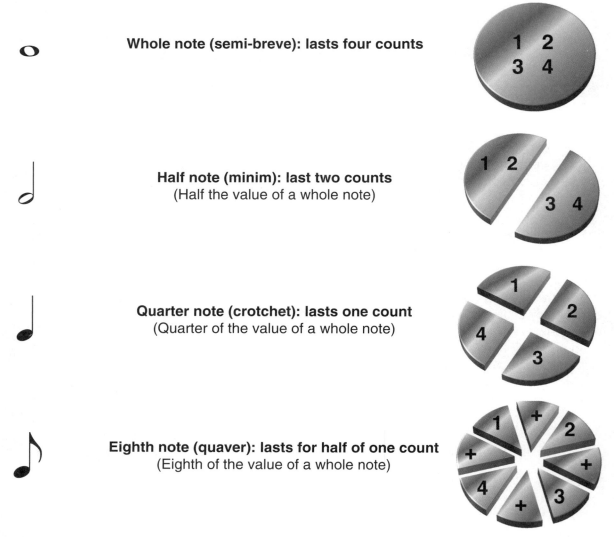

Whole note (semi-breve): lasts four counts

Half note (minim): last two counts
(Half the value of a whole note)

Quarter note (crotchet): lasts one count
(Quarter of the value of a whole note)

Eighth note (quaver): lasts for half of one count
(Eighth of the value of a whole note)

When we talk about a note lasting for several counts, you have to imagine the note being held as if you were blowing a trumpet. With a trumpet, the longer you blow, the longer the note lasts. With a drum there is no way to make a note last any longer than one hit, so we are therefore not actually holding the note or making it last, but instead just waiting for the correct amount of time until we play the next note.

Rests

Rests are symbols that tells us NOT to play anything for various durations. Every note has an equivelant rest with the same value. The next page explains each note and rest.

Note: Notes and rests do not join or run over the middle of a bar, this is why you will only see half notes and half note rests on counts one or three and eighth notes not joined across the middle of a bar.

Whole notes: four counts

Whole note:
Play a note that lasts four counts

Whole note rest:
DO NOT play anything for four counts

Half notes: two counts

Half notes:
Play a note that lasts two counts

Half note rests:
DO NOT play anything for two counts

Quarter notes: one count

Quarter notes:
Play a note that lasts one counts

Quarter note rests:
DO NOT play anything for one count

Eigth note: half of one count

Eighth notes:
Play a note that lasts half of one count

Eighth note rests:
DO NOT play anything for half of one count

Mixing basic note values and rests

The following snare drum exercises mix whole notes, half notes, quarter notes, eighth notes and rests.

Play each exercise separately and then play the whole page as one exercise.

Signing off and moving on
Play the entire page as one exercise with a click track
Targets are in BPM

60	65	70	75	80	85	90	95	100	105	110	115	120
Bronze						Silver						Gold

Fills with rests

Having now looked at several different note values and rests, here are some fills with rests which create some gaps in our playing. Sometimes leaving a space can sound better than filling every gap with lots of notes.

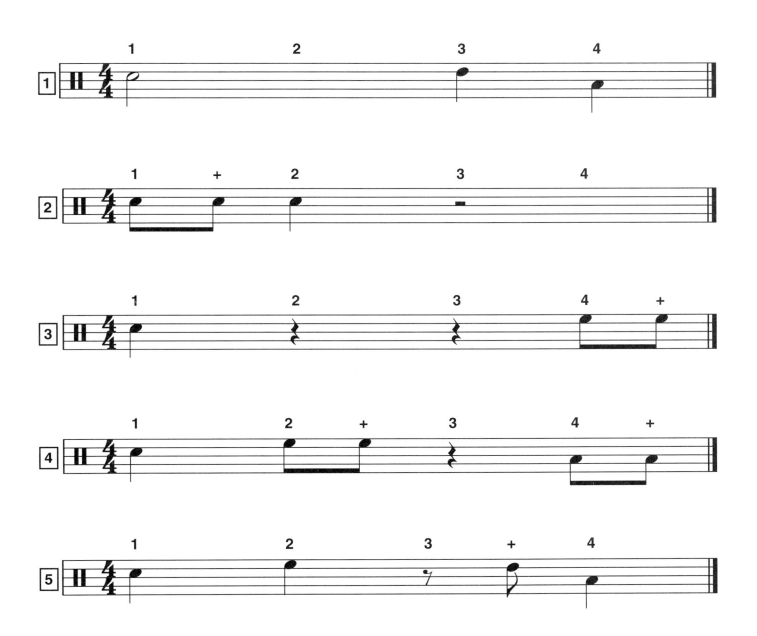

Signing off and moving on

Play each fill with the quarter or eighth note groove in four bar phrases along with suitable backing tracks
Targets are in BPM

60	65	70	75	80	85	90	95	100	105	110	115	120
Bronze					Silver					Gold		

Part bar fills

So far all of the fills we have looked at have taken up a whole bar, which is ideal when learning timing and counting, but is not always the most musical way to play. Although a fill will still quite often fall in the fourth bar, it does not have to take up the entire fourth bar, but instead can be just a part of the fourth bar.

The following three examples show alternatives to starting a fill on beat one of the fourth bar. Play four bar phrases using the eighth note groove and use each example as the fourth bar in a four bar phrase, making sure your count is nice and strong.

Signing off and moving on

Play each example with an eighth note groove in four bar phrases with suitable backing tracks
Targets are in BPM

60		65		70		75		80		85		90		95		100		105		110		115		120	
Bronze										Silver										Gold				

Four bar phrase practice

Over the next two pages we are going to put together everything we have learnt so far into some four bar phrases. Here you will see quarter notes, eighth notes, rests and part bar fills, and will use both hi-hats and ride cymbal within your grooves.

Play each four bar phrase slowly and remember to count as you go. When you feel confident enough, play along with backing tracks.

Signing off and moving on
Play each four bar phrase along with suitable backing tracks
Targets are in BPM

60		65	70	75	80	85	90	95	100	105	110	115	120
Bronze						Silver					Gold		

Four bar phrase practice continued

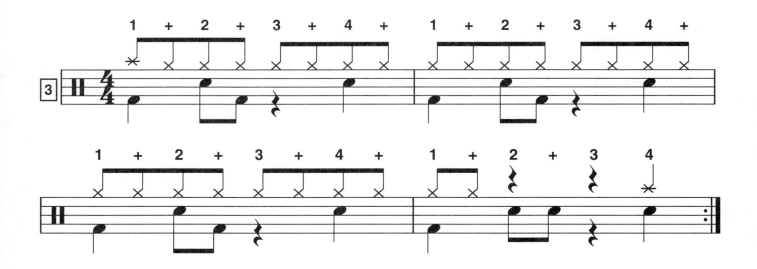

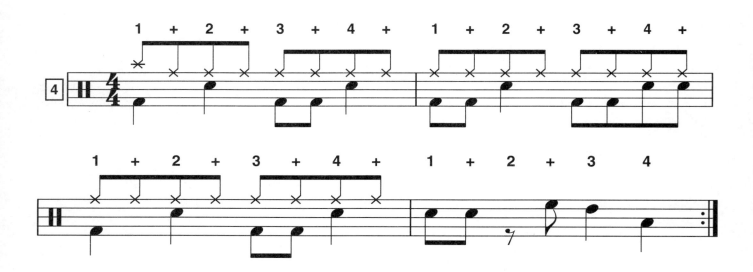

Signing off and moving on

Play each four bar phrase along with suitable backing tracks
Targets are in BPM

60	65	70	75	80	85	90	95	100	105	110	115	120
Bronze					Silver					Gold		

You gotta have style: Rock and Pop

As drummers, we know that we are responsible for keeping time for a band or group, but we are also musicians and need to understand about different types of music. We do not have to like every type of music, yet as musicians it is essential that we are aware and understand as much as we can about as many different types of music as possible.

Over the course of these books, we will look at several of the major styles of music that you should be aware of. It would be impossible to study each type of music in depth so instead there will be a brief summary of a styles history, main characteristics and some well known artists to check out.

To start with we will look at two styles of music that would suit the grooves and fills we have learnt so far, rock and pop!

Checklist

By the end of this chapter, you should be able to achieve the following:

- List some of the main characterstics of rock music
- List some of the main characterstics of pop music
- Identify if a song is a pop or a rock song
- Understand how you could adjust your playing to fit in with a pop or rock band

As in previous chapters, use this page as an end-of-chapter test. When you have completed Chapter Five, come back to this page and see if you can complete this list.

Rock music

History:
Rock music is one of the most popular styles of music around today with roots going right back to 1940s and 50s rock n roll, rhythm and blues and country music. It really entered the mainstream worldwide in the 1960s and has been around in many different forms ever since. The term 'rock n roll' was first used in the early 1950s.

Sound:
Generally, rock music can be identified by the sound of loud, raw electric guitars, pounding drums and bass guitar all topped off with strong anthemic vocals. Recordings tend to be less produced and polished which adds to the raw feel of the music. Bands are traditionally made up of between three to six musicians covering the roles of drummer, guitarist, bass player and vocalist. Extra musicians such as second guitarist and keyboard player are also very common but lots of different types of musicians have been involved with rock music over the years.

About:
Lots of young musicians that want to get out and play live in a group, form rock bands as it is relatively easy get started. Instruments needed are not always very expensive and you don't need to be a master of your instrument to make music and have fun. Those bands that stay together and go on to play bigger and better gigs (shows) may decide to play professionally, writing, recording and releasing albums as well as touring the country (or world!) playing for a living. Generally speaking rock bands are made up of a group of equal sharing musicians who write their own songs and play live shows. They write the music they love which is aimed at a certain fan base rather than trying to please a general audience.

Sub genres:
Rock music is a massive genre with lots of different styles within it. Some rock music is extremely heavy and loud, some is more produced and 'pop' like, some makes you feel happy and some makes you think. Here are just a few of the more popular sub genres of rock music you may come across:

Hard rock – Soft rock – Glam rock – Pop rock – Blues rock – Progressive rock – Punk rock - Alternative rock – Grunge – Goth rock – Electro rock – Garage rock – Folk rock – Psychedelic rock – Christian rock – Indie rock – Britpop

Recommended listening:
With a genre of music such as rock, there are so many artists covering so many periods and sub genres, it is impossible to write a short list that covers it all, so here are just a few to get you started.

The Kinks – The Rolling Stones – Led Zeppelin – Deep Purple – Pink Floyd – AC/DC – ZZ Top – Oasis – Nirvana – Muse – The Foo Fighters – Kaiser Chiefs – Queen – Red Hot Chilli Peppers – Van Halen

Signing off and moving on

List two characteristics of rock music, four instruments commonly used and two famous rock artists

Pop music

History:
Pop music is music which is created to be 'popular' and appeal to a wide audience. The term pop music was first used in the mid-1920s and ever since the 1950s has described any music which is popular with the youth of the day. Because of this, pop music has evolved massively as times and people have changed and has always followed current trends in music and fashion.

Sound:
As pop music is aimed at a much wider audience and aims to have mass appeal, it is quite often a lot softer and lighter than rock music. Instruments used in pop music can be similar to that of rock music but recordings are a lot more produced and instrument sounds are more controlled. More effects and samples can also be used to add to the overall polished sound. Songs are generally between two and a half and three and a half minutes long with a basic structure, simple melodies and catchy hooks. Traditionally, lyrics in pop songs quite often focus on simple themes such as love, romantic relationships and having fun.

About:
Although pop acts can be full bands or solo artists it is not unusual to have a third party responsible for writing their music for them. It is fairly common for record companies or producers to 'manufacture' pop groups by having carefully selected attractive singers perform songs written by top writers. The focus then tends to be more about the recordings and videos over live performance and about making money over creating art. This is not always the case though and there are lots of talented pop acts out there writing and recording their own songs and performing live.

Sub genres:
Pop is also a very broad genre with lots of different sub genres, here are just a few:

Dance pop – Electro pop – Techno pop – Teen pop – Pop rock – Pop punk - Bubblegum pop – Urban pop – Power pop – Disco – Pop rap – Boy bands – Girl bands – Sunshine pop – Euro pop – K pop – Indie pop

Recommended listening:
Just as with rock music, there are so many artists from so many periods and genres of pop music that a full list is impossible, here are just a few artists to get you started:

Frank Sinatra – The Beatles – Elton John – Michael Jackson – Duran Duran – Wham – Kylie Minogue Take That – Madonna – Britney Spears – Robbie Williams – Spice Girls – Lady Ga Ga – Ellie Goulding

Signing off and moving on

List two characteristics of pop music, two sub genres of pop and two famous pop artists

Playing rock and pop music

Over the previous two pages we have looked at rock and pop music and although all of the grooves and fills from this book will work with either style, it is how we play them that will make them sound different. Generally, rock music has a louder, more raw feel to it, whereas pop music is more controlled and cleaner. If we approach the drum kit like this, we can make our playing fit in with either style even if the grooves and fills look the same written down.

By using different parts of the drum stick and by playing different parts of your drums and cymbals, you can drastically change the sounds created. Here are a few suggestions to help you change the sound of your drums to fit in with the music you are playing.

Shaft of the stick: Most of the time when playing the hi-hats, you will hit the side of the hi-hats with the shaft of the stick. This is a very strong yet relaxed way to play and gets a fuller sound from the hi-hats. Playing harder will get you more volume and playing softer will reduce the volume.

Shaft of the stick

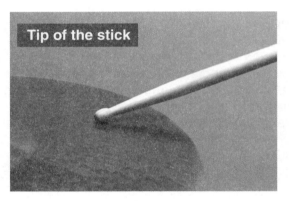
Tip of the stick

Tip of the stick: To get a tighter, more controlled sound, you could try playing on the top or very edge of the hi-hats with the tip of the stick. This is not such a natural way to play but will help keep the volume of your hi-hats down and create a more pop like feel.

Centre of the drum: So far, all of our snare drum hits should have been with the tip of the stick hitting just off centre of the snare drum. This is the most natural way to play and gets the best sound from the drum. By striking the snare drum with the drum stick starting at different heights you can get different volumes and therefore different sounds. Try keeping the tip of the stick close to the snare drum to get a lighter sound.

Centre of the drum
Rim shot

Rim shots: To create a very powerful and loud snare drum sound, you can play what is known as a rim shot. This is a strike where the shaft of the stick hits the rim of the drum at the same time as the tip of the stick hits the centre of the snare drum. This is sometimes too overpowering to use all of the time though.

To hear for yourself how much of a difference these small changes can make, try the following:
1. Play along to a rock song hitting the hi-hats with the shaft of the stick, rim shots on the snare drum and heel up bass drum technique.

2. Play along to a pop song hitting the hi-hats with the tip of the stick, the snare drum in the centre of the drum and use the heel down bass drum technique.

End of the beginning

Having now worked through this book, you should have a basic understanding of your role as a drummer, how the drum kit works as a musical instrument and a time-keeping tool, and how music is written.

Checklist

Having now completed chapters one to five, you should now be able to achieve the following:

- Understand and explain the role of a drummer
- Read, play and write basic grooves and fills
- Understand and read note values and rests
- Play in time with music
- Demonstrate good technique and posture
- Play basic rudiments

This is the final chapter and brings together everything you have learnt so far. If you struggle on any aspect within these last few pages, you may need to refer back to previous chapters to refresh your memory. Have fun and good luck!

Grade exams

If you are interested in taking exams in music, you have now covered enough material to take a 'debut' or 'beginner' (pre-grade one) exam. Talk to your teacher about what you need to do after completing this final chapter.

Drum charts

A chart is an entire song or piece of music written out in notation and is like a map for a song telling you what to play for each section. A drum chart can be for snare drum or full drum kit, and may well contain repeat markings and other information.

Charting success

Over the next few pages there are several charts, which need to be played with either a click track or a backing track. Take your time to look over these charts and work through each one slowly before attempting to play with backing tracks or click tracks. When playing these charts use your ears, don't concentrate so much on reading that your timing suffers. Remember a drummer's job is to keep time, it's better to make a few mistakes but keep perfect time than to get every note correct but play out of time!

Backing tracks for full drum kit are provided in two formats:

• Backing track with drum track
• Backing track with click

To sign off each chart you should play along with the backing track with click track. Snare drum pieces should be played with the click tracks provided (tracks 20 to 32 on your CD). Start slowly and gradually increase the tempo as you gain confidence.

Chart One: basic note values

This first chart is for the snare drum, and contains basic notes and rests.

Count in: 1 - 2 - 1-2-3-4

Signing off and moving on

Play the entire chart with a click track

Targets are in BPM

60	65	70	75	80	85	90	95	100	105	110	115	120
Bronze						Silver						Gold

Chart Two: quarter note rock (100bpm)

Track 14: With drums
Track 15: With click

Count in: 1 - 2 - 1-2-3-4

Repeat previous bar

Double bar line - End of section

Signing off and moving on
Play the chart with backing track Number 15

Gold: Good timing and no mistakes
Silver: Good timing and with three or fewer mistakes
Bronze: Acceptable timing with three or fewer mistakes

Chart Three: eighth note pop (80bpm)

Track 16: With drums
Track 17: With click

Count in: 1 - 2 - 1-2-3-4

Signing off and moving on

Play the chart with backing track Number 17

Gold: Good timing and no mistakes
Silver: Good timing and with three or fewer mistakes
Bronze: Acceptable timing with three or fewer mistakes

Chart Four: mixed rhythm rock (90bpm)

Track 18: With drums
Track 19: With click

Count in: 1 - 2 - 1-2-3-4

Signing off and moving on
Play the chart with backing track Number 19

Gold: Good timing and no mistakes
Silver: Good timing and with three or fewer mistakes
Bronze: Acceptable timing with three or fewer mistakes

End of book test

Fill in the blanks below and then check your answers over the page.

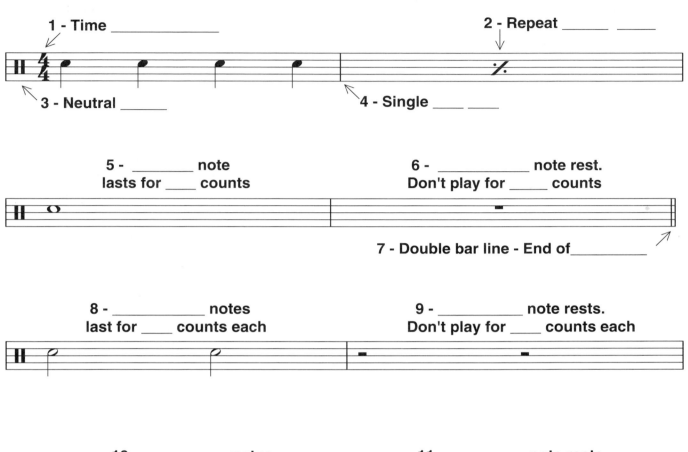

1 - Time _____

2 - Repeat _____ ____

3 - Neutral _____

4 - Single ____ ____

5 - _____ note
lasts for ____ counts

6 - _____ note rest.
Don't play for _____ counts

7 - Double bar line - End of_____

8 - _____ notes
last for ____ counts each

9 - _____ note rests.
Don't play for ____ counts each

10 - _____ notes
last for ____ count each

11 - _____ note rests.
Don't play for ___ count each

12 - Start _____

13 - _____ Repeat

15 - _____ notes
lasts for ____ of one count each

15 - _____ note rests.
Don't play for ___ of one count each

16 - Final barline - End of _____

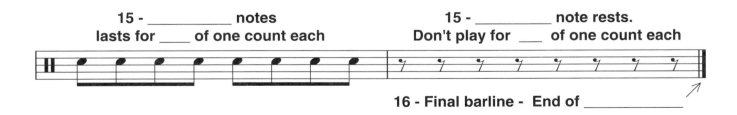

17: A drummers job is to………………………………………

18: A paradiddle sticking is………………………………………

End of book test: answers

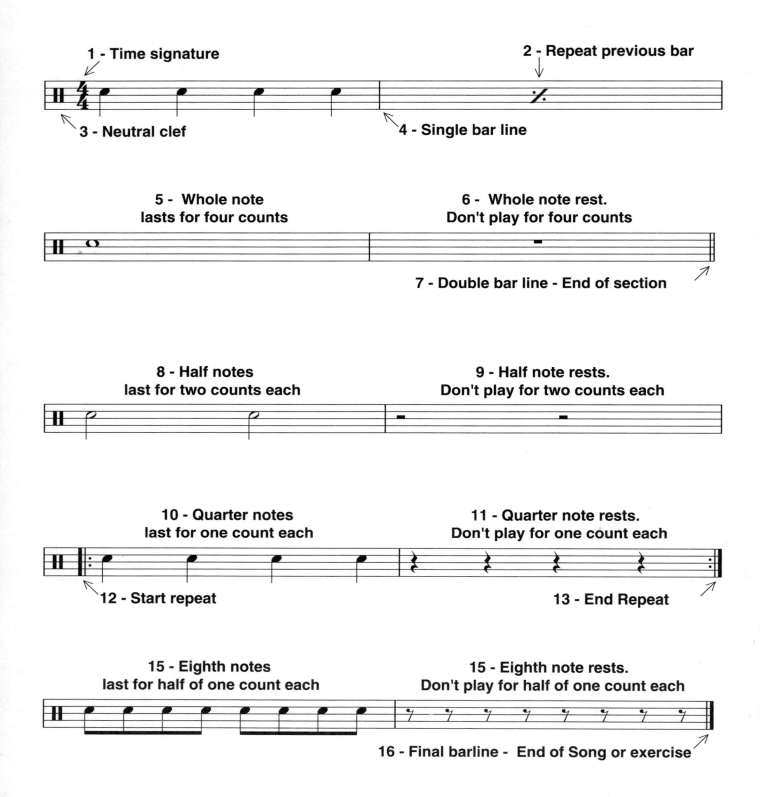

1 - Time signature

2 - Repeat previous bar

3 - Neutral clef

4 - Single bar line

5 - Whole note lasts for four counts

6 - Whole note rest. Don't play for four counts

7 - Double bar line - End of section

8 - Half notes last for two counts each

9 - Half note rests. Don't play for two counts each

10 - Quarter notes last for one count each

11 - Quarter note rests. Don't play for one count each

12 - Start repeat

13 - End Repeat

15 - Eighth notes last for half of one count each

15 - Eighth note rests. Don't play for half of one count each

16 - Final barline - End of Song or exercise

17: A drummers job is to: Keep time for a band

18: A paradiddle sticking is: R L R R L R L L